My Dearest Daughters
from Mom, with love

Lady Schowanda M. Michael

Lady Schowanda Michael
1011 N. Bon Marche Drive
Baton Rouge, LA 70806

ladyschowandamichael@gmail.com
(225) 681-3538

Edited by Travail Publishing

Printed in the United States of America

All scriptures are taken from the KING JAMES VERSION unless otherwise noted.

Scriptures marked NIV are taken from the NEW INTERNATIONAL VERSION (NIV): Scripture taken from THE HOLY BIBLE, NEW INTERNATIONAL VERSION ®. Copyright© 1973, 1978, 1984, 2011 by Biblica, Inc.™. Used by permission of Zondervan

Scriptures marked NLT are taken from the HOLY BIBLE, NEW LIVING TRANSLATION (NLT): Scriptures taken from the HOLY BIBLE, NEW LIVING TRANSLATION, Copyright© 1996, 2004, 2007 by Tyndale House Foundation. Used by permission of Tyndale House Publishers, Inc., Carol Stream, Illinois 60188. All rights reserved. Used by permission.

ISBN-10: 1542349281
ISBN-13: 978-1542349284

DEDICATION

I would like to first dedicate *My Dearest Daughters* to my daughters, Carion and Carielle who have supported me and given up their mother unselfishly.

To all of the women who mentored me throughout my life and helped to guide me to become the Woman of God that I am today, I dedicate this book to you…my mom, Marva Bowser; .who is the epitome of strength. She is my She-Ro; Barbara Chopin, my mother in law whom I love dearly; Doris Michael, Jackie Storks, Barbara Franklin, Betty Foster, Lula Bell, Lola Davis, and my Aunt Ella Mae Davis.

To Beatrice Mitchell, my Spiritual Mother; thank you for all of your mentoring. You saw something in me when I didn't see it in myself.

To all of the women who surround me on a daily basis, I love you with all my heart!

CONTENTS

ACKNOWLEDGMENTS

I would like to take the time to thank my husband of 26 years and counting, Cardell, Sr. for his love, support and his belief in the gift that God entrusted me with; my sons, Cardell, Jr. and Caron, you are not forgotten. My next book *My Dearest Sons*, is dedicated to you and to my daughter-in-law, Corteiona, I love you.

I would also like to thank my siblings, Belissa Davis, Coty Miller, Roy Miller, Sr. and Demetrius Miller, Sr. each of you were instrumental in my life.

Wanda Burns, one of my spiritual daughters, thank you for helping me fulfill my dream.

Preface
A Spiritual Mother

What is a "Spiritual Mother"? She is one who is commissioned for the work! A spiritual mother is one who supernaturally cares for the souls of God's children and requires maturity for them. A spiritual mother is not self-seeking, nor is she biased. She is longsuffering and has temperance. She is meek, loving, patient and kind. She walks according to the will of the Father. Her maternal instinct will nurture divine life in others. A spiritual mother spends much time caring for people, whether related by blood or not. She will find herself always teaching, nurturing and praying.

When Deborah was commissioned to do the work, she did not complain, but instead, she stood and rose to the task set before her by God. Who was Deborah? Her name means "bee". A bee is ranked the highest in intelligence within the animal kingdom. Deborah was a prophetess, a judge and a spiritual mother to Israel. She did more than prophesy; she moved a nation that was in depths of despair by her fearless and unwavering devotion to the freeing of God's people. She awoke in the people a desire to be free from bondage. She was one that produced change with the many gifts given to her by God to inspire others. Deborah lived in a time where the land was ruined by its oppressors, the Canaanites. Her people were afraid and their spirits were broken.

I chose to write this book to bring hope, joy, and inspiration to the hearts and minds of God's daughters. *My Dearest Daughters* is for you! Whether biological, spiritual or through adoption (not of the fold) this book has been written with you in mind and I hope that it will impact your life tremendously. I believe that these power-packed letters from my personal experience of survival, triumphs, defeats, and victories will influence your life with hope, inspiration, and motivation.

I desire that all who read this book will come to know and understand the principals of life's journey as a spiritual mother. As you journey through each letter, I have provided space for you to journal your thoughts and feelings. It is my prayer that you will grow in the grace and knowledge of our Lord and Savior, Jesus Christ. *2 Peter 3:18*, says, **But grow in grace, and in the knowledge of our Lord and Saviour Jesus Christ. To him be the glory both now and forever. Amen**

This could be a book of journaling for you leave to your daughter(s) or your loved one(s) to help aid them in tough times. I know that we would hope that we would be there always to inspire, to encourage as well as to motivate, but time is not promised to any of us. Do not put off for tomorrow what can be done today. Live, love and learn. These journals will serve as a resounding voice of God's word.

To my own daughters, I would like to leave a legacy of faith through the words of encouragement that lies within the pages of these letters. You, my daughter, are stronger than you believe. You are better than where you are at this moment. Being a child from The Ponderosa, a small place called Convent, I used to to believe that my opportunities were limited but I now realize that my opportunities were innumerable. My only limitation was how I saw things until I was shown something greater within myself.

CHAPTER 1

WHEN LIFE SEEMS TO SPIN
OUT OF CONTROL

My Dearest Daughter,

When life seems to spin out of control; when it seems you have taken a misstep; when it seems you have driven too far off course; when it seems you have walked too long on the same path and nothing seems to change; when it seems as if you have thought too hard on the same situation and it has driven you up a wall; when it seems as though you have come to a point of no return and that point seems to have spiraled in all directions, it is at that moment, I want you to know that you can make it! You will make it! All it will take is one more step by you; just one more!

I am reminded of a moment when I used to spin my daughters around and around. Of course, this was a time when I could have handled being turned around repeatedly. The body, through time and changes, I just cannot do some of the things I used to do anymore!

I know we all can relate to a memory, one where you have been turned around by someone or something. If you have been to a state fair and rode one of those rides that spins you around or went to the park and got onto the spinning top, etc. One way or another you have experienced some level of turning around until you became dizzy. Even if you stood in one place and turned around and around on your own, I believe you get the picture of "spinning out of control".

In those moments my daughters and I would laugh so hard that we were brought to tears. But, it came to a point where I let go of their hands and began to feel the effects of turning them around and around so much to where I was dizzy and overwhelmed with a gushing feeling inside of my stomach. As I tried focusing really hard upon my daughter, I could see them trying to get their balance while trying to get across the room to me. I would try moving quickly to pick them up at the same time giggling and stumbling along the way. Of course, you know they wanted to go again and again until our heads and stomachs from the pain and nausea could take no more.

Isn't it funny how life is? A harmless game seems so fun and innocent. If life was only like the game then the present situation would be over quicker than it started. Your stomach would quickly stop aching, the room would stop spinning, your equilibrium would function properly and immediately you would laugh. You are certain to encounter in life, the issues of the heart.

Daughter, whether by birth or spiritual, my heart's desire is that you will make sense of where you are right now and that you will not look through the eyes of doubt, loss or fear but build yourself up in the way that's pleasing to God. Keep your heart fixed on the will of the Father (God). Keep your heart untangled in regrets that will send you into an emotional breakdown. We are commanded by the Father to, "*above all else to guard our heart*," not the mass in the middle of our breastplate but the thinker inside of us. The emotional part of us holds on to everything, whether good, bad or indifferent. The scripture goes on to say, "*for this shall determine the outcome of life*". The outcome is where we are right now, daughter. You can make it through it! It is your choice. **Lean not to your own understanding (Proverbs 3:5)** but let the wisdom of God pierce your conscious and unconscious thoughts with His wisdom to give direction in your life.

With this first letter of personal reflection, I want you to understand that God's deepest desire for your life is always greater than where you are right now. Your right now may not look promising to you because everything

4

seems to be spinning out of control but I want you to know that God is able. With your next step, let it determine your greater outcome. Choose wisely for the choice has always been yours. You are older now, no longer the little girl that momma can pick up and spin around. The time of maturity is now. The time of your breakthrough is now. The time to let go of what's trying to control you or you trying to control it, is now.

Just as we spun around and around for a time and I released your hand that you may be able find your own balance again, it is the same way you must do for yourself now. Let go! Your eyes have been opened to the ways of the world but the most important thing is for your heart to be open to the will of the Father.

I know you can make it!

Prayer of Agreement:

Father, in the name of Jesus, I ask for your forgiveness to come into my heart of all sins committed against my body and mind. I pray for and receive your wisdom and guidance. Father, I welcome your guidance and touch upon my life. I pray for the kingdom to influence me that my unconscious and conscious thought will be purified from all dead works right now, in the name of Jesus! *–Amen*

Reflection Scripture:

Guard your heart above all else, for everything you do flows from it. ~ **Proverbs 4:23**

My Personal Journal Notes:

_____

_____

_____

_____

_____

_____

_____

_____

_____

_____

_____

_____

_____

_____

_____

_____

_____

_____

_____

_____

_____

_____

_____

Signed: _____

Date: _____

My Personal Journal Notes:

_____

_____

_____

_____

_____

_____

_____

_____

_____

_____

_____

_____

_____

_____

_____

_____

_____

_____

_____

_____

_____

_____

_____

Signed: _____

Date: _____

My Personal Journal Notes:

_____

_____

_____

_____

_____

_____

_____

_____

_____

_____

_____

_____

_____

_____

_____

_____

_____

_____

_____

_____

_____

_____

_____

_____

Signed: _____

Date: _____

CHAPTER 2

WHEN YOU HAVE FALLEN

My Dearest Daughter,

When it seems like you have fallen and can't get up, remember these words, "you can make it." If I have not told you before I'm telling you now that there will be difficult times in your life that you will feel like not going on but you must. You must continue the journey that has been set for you.

Life will not always seem fair. Life will not always be fair. In some cases, justice will be nowhere to be found. It will seem as if everything and everyone is against you. Sometimes it may even seem like the world is upon your shoulders but at that moment…breathe!

I'm reminded of times when my natural daughter fell down and scratched their knees, hands and elbows on many occasions. Once, one of them fell so hard that she broke her arm or shall I say she was pushed by another kid that caused her arm to be broken. As she was falling she tried to brace herself by putting her arm in the way causing a breakage in two places which resulted in a cast. This extended from her elbow to her hand and had to be worn for six months. When the cast was removed her skin peeled consistently for weeks. It had shrunken smaller than the other arm, smelled a little funny at first and was discolored and fragile. Initially, she found herself consistently using the other arm more than the one that was broken because she was in fear she would break it again. Fear almost cost her to get comfortable with the limitation of one limb.

What am I saying? I'm saying that sometimes in life we will fall and some falls will be harder than the others. Some falls will take place in your life that may have been caused by others. Right here is where it is most important not to use excuses to remain in a place or shall I say, in a fallen state. What do I mean by fallen? I mean in a place of brokenness; a place that you can surrender consciously or unconsciously and that will keep you in a perpetual place of pain. In this place there are mirrors of reflections of pain and memories that will try to haunt you even in your awakened hours. I hear the word of the Lord saying to you right now daughter, "Be ye set free", says, the Lord.

Galatians 5:1 Stand fast therefore in the liberty wherewith Christ hath made us free, and be not entangled again with the yoke of bondage.

The choice of freedom is yours. I am assured that you will make the right decision in this hour of your life. Set sail, soar like an eagle and be courageous like the ant that can lift 5,000 times its own body weight.

It is only for this moment and time will heal all wounds. It will get better and the pain is only temporary. It may seem like you will not trust, love, learn, or experience again in life but I'm telling you that you can and you will overcome! You are an overcomer! You will get through it as you are recovering from the emotional, mental, physical and/or financial scars of life.

Remember, there is nothing new under the sun. If It has happening to you, it has already happened to someone else. The bible says in, *Ecclesiastes 1:9 (NIV) - What has been will be again, what has been done will be done again; there is nothing new under the sun.* Why do I tell you this? Because I do not want you to feel like you are the ONLY one in the world going through what you are going through. What is pain? Pain is physical suffering or discomfort caused by illness or injury: What is psychological or mental pain? It is an unpleasant feeling (a suffering). Pain aids as a reminder of what has taken place in your life. Holding on to this type of pain will cause you to feel overwhelmed and to suffer needlessly which will turn into depression. The technical terms include algopsychalia and psychalgia, but it may also be called mental pain, emotional pain, psychic pain, social pain, spiritual or soul pain, or suffering.

My Dearest Daughter, letting go in order to rebuild your life is the key to getting up from your fall. My desire is not to take you to school but only to provide understanding by schooling you with the wisdom that's needful to survive life by not becoming a victim. There are two scriptures I would like to share with you right now so that you may know that God will always be that present help in your time of need.

Psalm 18:2 (NIV) says, The Lord is my rock and my fortress and my deliverer, my God, my rock, in whom I take refuge, my shield, and the horn of my salvation, my stronghold.

Psalm 34:18 (NLV) says, The Lord is near to the brokenhearted and saves the crushed in spirit.

Fear will only hinder your progress. Fear will cause you to get into a comfortable place of life and freeze you in time. Daughter, do not allow this no matter how difficult it is. You can make it. You are not alone. In my closing letter to you, my birth and spiritual daughter, remember you are a winner, right now! Let us pray together.

Prayer of Agreement:

Father, in the name of your precious son, Jesus Christ, the anointed one, we come in a Prayer of Agreement that you keep us in perfect peace. Father, in the name of Jesus, with all knowledge and wisdom on your side because we know that you know the plans for our lives we thank you for being the present help. Forgive us for unspoken thoughts that we have allowed to settle within us that only marked our grave. For you are Alpha and Omega. For you are our shield and buckler. For you are our healer of our broken hearts. Father, right now we speak life into our lives and we receive the abundant flow of your overpowering joy, comfort, peace and serenity. Thank you Lord! -*Amen*

Reflection Scripture:

"I have told you these things, so that in me (Jesus) you may have peace. In this world you will have trouble. But take heart! I have overcome the world." ~ **John 16:33**

My Personal Journal Notes:

_____

_____

_____

_____

_____

_____

_____

_____

_____

_____

_____

_____

_____

_____

_____

_____

_____

_____

_____

_____

_____

_____

_____

Signed: _____

Date: _____

My Personal Journal Notes:

_____

_____

_____

_____

_____

_____

_____

_____

_____

_____

_____

_____

_____

_____

_____

_____

_____

_____

_____

_____

_____

_____

_____

Signed: _____

Date: _____

My Personal Journal Notes:

_____

_____

_____

_____

_____

_____

_____

_____

_____

_____

_____

_____

_____

_____

_____

_____

_____

_____

_____

_____

_____

_____

_____

Signed: _____

Date: _____

CHAPTER 3

THIS MAY BE A ROUGH ONE

My Dearest Daughter,

I am writing this with you in mind. Whether I am here in the natural, the present or in the spirit, this letter is just for you. When you begin to read this letter it will seem like I know and feel exactly what you are going through. It is only by God's grace and mercy that we are here at this point today. He still has a plan. He still has a purpose. He still has a mandate for your life. You must know and recognize this important message of life right now before we move forward because this may be a rough one that you may feel you cannot overcome. Lean back. Breathe.

You have been dreading a day like today for a long time. You are at the point where you can't take it anymore and to top it all off this one came as a total surprise leaving you speechless! Just when you thought everything was going good with you, here goes something else trying to disrupt your peace. No, daughter this isn't a dream, there is no hole to fall into, this is really happening right now! You will endure, persevere, press through, overcome and manage your breathing by managing your emotions. Your commitment to life, family and most importantly God, will not allow you to fail or run away!

Well, I have something important to say and you need to pull up your best chair, put your best song on with your favorite blanket or fuzzy slippers, your best cup of coffee, a box of tissues and get into a comfortable place. That place may be a park bench, front seat of your car, in your bedroom, soaking in a tub of bubbles with the candles lit, it does not matter. My point is… just steal away by yourself for moment. You will be thankful later. Whatever or wherever you need to get, get there so we can began our journey back, so I can share with you some heartfelt promises and wisdom points of life that got me through and to the "but God moment"!

In the early stages of my baby daughter's life, six months in she began to breakout with rashes on her body. We found out later that she had a severe case of eczema with an acute sensitivity to water which caused a burning sensation all over her body. If that was not enough to try and comprehend, she developed a problem with breathing that resulted in asthma and hospitalization. We will discuss this later.

Now, you have to understand, we have a new baby. She is our fourth child and we are super excited. Life is moving on as planned and suddenly, this issue begins to arise. Her body reacted to heat, foods and certain drinks (that we found out much later) that caused breakouts on her body. You can imagine at six months how miserable she had to be as an infant. Stuck with no way to communicate verbally, leaving her hollering and crying in misery. Can you imagine being a parent and not knowing what to do or how to help? There is a feeling of helplessness and sometimes you find yourself blaming yourself. Could I have done something differently? Should I have eaten or drank more of this or less of that? It felt like I was a new parent all over again with no experience on how to raise a child.

I could see and understand that we were headed into a rough one. To see someone you love go through something that you do not understand and you want to help but do not know how to help only to find out later when she could finally talk some of the things you were doing was causing more pain and misery. Just a simple thing as bath time! Gosh, what a horrible feeling to know the pain you were administering and did not know.

There were many sleepless nights, many remedies new and old but nothing seemed to help. The emotional toll was hard and demanding at times so there was no room for me to soak in my own emotions of self-loathing. Why? Because she needed me. The family needed me so there was no time for that. I cried out many times to God for help, understanding and an answer.

Limited by her little arms, she could not reach every sensitive area of her body to scratch. You can imagine the many doctor visits we went to only to come out with the same answer…heat rash, use topical cream and steroids. All of those remedies would soothe the body for a while but before long it was back again…the constant crying, agony, pain, discoloration of the skin, etc. Sometimes we would even think that was just her wanting attention and it was no way it could be that bad. Sadly, it really was that bad. Her skin began to swell around her neck because of the deep laceration from her nails cutting into her skin. Now, I see a child totally bound to the sofa. Not walking much anymore and when she was made to walk she would crawl on the floor because of the swelling behind her knees due to deep lacerations.

Our ultimate test was weeping of the skin. Her skin would weep constantly. She refused to wear short sleeves or pants. One time we were on vacation and I remember the family trying to get her to come out and get into pool and play with the other kids. She refused! The more we aggravated her to come out the more she got upset. Later we tried to bath her for the night and my baby (about seven years old) screamed and that scream shook me to my core. I looked into her eyes and saw the pain, the hurt but most of all I saw my baby about to lose her mind. This was my turning point and I said enough, I'm tired of seeing her going through this. Something must be done. The next morning I took her to the emergency room in New Orleans looking for answers and refusing to leave without any. Immediately, when the nurses saw her they admitted her right away and the healing process began.

Breathe! This was the first time in a long time I was able to do that for real. From the age of 6 months to almost eight years old she suffered. Now she was hospitalized for five days due to staph infections. It was here that I received so many answers that I had been praying for. She received the proper treatment and we now had an understanding from all the research that I had been doing on my own.

After several tests, we found out that she was allergic to many foods and drinks. They sent us to specialists at St.

Jude because they thought she may have had cancer because of the enlarge lymph nodes around her neck. They found that her lymph nodes were enlarged because of her constantly scratching her neck. A few weeks before this I remember getting a word from a prophet that said, "the Spirit of the Lord says, to have her to take communion for so many days." We began doing accordingly. We came together as a family and prayed for her. My daughter would make her way to the church bookstore and requested a box of communion for her to continue the process. Now that was amazing! This was one of the roughest roads we had to travel as a family but we made it through and to our "but God moment!".

My dearest daughter, in the midst of everything you may be facing I want you to know there is a "but God" moment for you too! Jehovah-Shammah...the Lord is there! Our God is already in your tomorrow. He already knows what your future looks like and He has complete control over it. We are told in **Jeremiah 29:11 (NLT)**, **"For I know the plans I have for you," says the Lord. "They are plans for good and not for disaster, to give you a future and a hope".** The Lord is there!

You cannot be in control of your future now, but He can. Jehovah-Shammah will walk with you into whatever tomorrow holds because of His great plan and love for you. God is there in your tomorrow and in my tomorrow. He simply desires that we trust His plan. I know for a fact that if it was not for God being in the midst that I would have lost it so many times. I want you to know this, I was not scripture chunky as a matter of fact, I was very new in the word. But I still believed. I still believed God no matter what. It caused me to grow closer to Him. You may say, WOW why did it take so long? I cannot answer this for you because I do not know why but I know that it had purpose. Without these moments, we would not have the strength to overcome obstacles that come our way.

You are filled with mixed emotions, wanting to scream rather than smile, wanting to exchange places rather than to overcome, wanting to stop rather than to experience in order to recover, wanting to let go rather than remain and learn to gain the promises and wisdom of God. Fulfillment comes in funny ways…ways that we cannot seem to imagine but nevertheless it comes. Receive it when comes. Embrace it when it shows up. Stand on it.

What is fulfillment? Fulfillment is the satisfaction or

happiness as a result of fully developing one's abilities or character; the achievement of something desired, promised, or predicted; the meeting of a requirement or condition; the performance of a task, duty, or role as required, pledged, or expected. Through your pain and discomfort I want you to know that there is a "but God" moment for you, too." A moment when you relize that He never left and He was there all the time – But God!

Prayer of Agreement:

Father, in the name of Jesus, I bless you. I give you glory. Father, I thank you now and forever for being Jehovah-Shammah, the God who is with us. I thank you that you are my Jehovah-Shalom, the God of peace. Father, forgive me Lord, for the moment when I began the process of going through and I did not realize that it would all work together for my good. Forgive me, Lord for the moment that I allowed fear to cancel my faith. Father, forgive me for this has been a rough journey; rougher than I have ever experienced. But, today I surrender all conscious and unconscious thoughts unto you right now in the name of Jesus and I pray that you will take full control of my life. I surrender unto you every pain, every situation, every heart issue in Jesus' name. *Amen*

Reflection Scripture:

For I know the plans I have for you," says the Lord. "They are plans for good and not for disaster, to give you a future and a hope". ~ *Jeremiah 29:11*

My Personal Journal Notes:

_____

_____

_____

_____

_____

_____

_____

_____

_____

_____

_____

_____

Signed: _____

Date: _____

My Personal Journal Notes:

Signed: _____

Date: _____

My Personal Journal Notes:

_____

_____

_____

_____

_____

_____

_____

_____

_____

_____

_____

_____

_____

_____

_____

_____

_____

_____

_____

_____

_____

_____

_____

_____

_____

_____

_____

Signed: _____

Date: _____

CHAPTER 4

WAIT

My Dearest Daughter,

While you wait! Waiting, within itself, can be very tricky. According to Webster's dictionary, we understand waiting to mean to stay where one is or to delay action until a particular time or until something else happens. Wait is one of the most dreaded words you would want to hear but nevertheless, some things in life cause you to wait, to halt in that place, even if that place is discomfort. Questions will form inside of your thought process while you are waiting for a fraction of time for anything. It stirs up many emotions that will cause conflict within oneself. This will be one of your greatest 'why me' moments. Why do I always have to wait? Why can't I get off this path? Why is everything so hard for me? Why can't I achieve success? Why are people always leaving me? Why? Why? Do not let it get the best of you. Waiting doesn't always have to be a bad thing but I know it can be a difficult thing to do. Daughter, I know the best is yet come for you!

When my moment of waiting came, time seemed to stand still and I thought that I would never leave that place. In this place I was burdened down, stressed, tormented and fought many battles in my mind. While I waited, in what seemed to be a long, cold, dark and lonely place was actually a small fraction of time. If I could prevent you from getting into this place, I would. I'm using one of the most powerful tools I know at this moment to talk you through the place that gives no comfort; the place that renders no sleep; the place that you do not understand; the place where time stands still.

My Dearest Daughters, have you ever been so overjoyed about something that it took your breath away? Have you ever been at that place of happiness where life seems grand? Have you ever been in that place of total peace where it seems like nothing CAN STOP YOU NOW? Have you ever loved before and thought that it was the ultimate thing and nothing could ever get in the way? Hmmmmm. Have you? Well, I have!

In my moment of 'WAIT' it happened so suddenly…infidelity! This moment came before the birth of oldest son. My husband and I were just six months into our marriage-newlyweds. Before I could understand my role as a wife it happened. WAIT -Now I don't know if God was looking for a good opportunity, but I know one had presented itself and it was no way I was going to make it without Him. Sometimes, daughters, you will find that your greatest achievement of growth will come in your moments of WAIT. In waiting, this is where I found my growth, which resulted in maturity. When you let God be God, you will emerge out of the cave brand spanking new.

Until the moment of my WAIT, feelings of rejection and pain crept in so quickly and bit me right on my bottom. There were so many questions, so many thoughts, and so many disappointments with one ultimate question, WHAT DO I DO NOW? This moment tested everything, even my love. The best way I can explain this experience is by asking you to picture me standing in my kitchen, washing a glass when suddenly it slips out of my and SHATTERS all over the floor bringing my perfect world to a HALT – A WAIT. You have to understand, I did not ask for this; I never expected this; I never desired this. NOW WHAT?

Looking at my life, which seemed like a thousand pieces of shattered pieces and shards of broken glass, I began questioning myself. How do I begin again? Where do I start to pick up the pieces to where I do not cause more damage? Can I survive this? Will I make through? What did I do to deserve this? Then I would answer myself…Yes, you desired it. Now look at me, confused, hurt, empty, heartbroken, lonely. Within, I felt abandoned although he never left. So many things were swirling around in my head constantly. In public, I smiled to keep from crying. I felt no peace and there was no joy in sight. It was all gone and I would never, ever be that happy again…so I thought.

I constantly warred within myself and kept constant company with pain, rejection, guilt, hatred, rage, etc., etc., etc. You name it; I went there in thought. My wait was hard until my 'GOD ENCOUNTER' where He first taught me how to forgive for real. In forgiving for real, my healing process began. This encounter changed my life forever. God began to cleanse me from the inside out. The process seemed like it took forever but I made through and guess what? You can too. It may not be this issue that will try to cause your WAIT, but whatever your issue is, know that you will SURVIVE YOUR WAIT! Where I was only looking to be a wife and to be loved, God took an opportunity through my pain and showed me how to BECOME so much more in my WAIT!

My wait was and has always been a lesson of maturity. I have gone through many seasons and battles of waiting and the results have always been the same and that was me maturing and becoming better than who I was at that moment. The same shines through for you today. When you entered into this place you may have been a little headstrong, no patience, a know-it-all, hot headed, short tempered, no compassion, no confidence, etc. You were so busy looking through dim glass that you could not recognize your own reflection staring right at you. It has always been the man in the mirror that God always wants to get right, not the man, woman, or child across the room. It has always been you!

We can go through our many scars some of which are so deep that some of us will always have them as a part of us until we leave this earth. The only difference with remembering and seeing the scar is that it you are no longer bound by the pain. Remember, it is not about that person being right or wrong, it is about you! It has always been about you. Whose life are you living right now? I can answer that for you – yours! When you awake in the morning and look into the mirror who do you see? Yes, you are right - you! It is all about you.

I have come to realize that we all have experiences and challenges in our lives. Some of us live through it and mature to tell you about it while others languish (remain) in that place. My 'growing up' was not always easy but I know that it was worth it.

So, as I pen my heartfelt thoughts to get you through that place of waiting, where time seems to have stood still, read this letter with the mindset that, "I will go through and I will not allow it to put me in a coffin which is also known as my place of burial." What caused the halt in your life? Most of the time it is pain. Now, this pain can be due to death of a close loved one; due to heartbreak; due to no direction, due to yearning for something more. This pain may come from someone who has harmed you sexually, verbally or physically. I know I have been there and I clawed my way up and out of the pit that was meant to kill me. In the past I have had regrets. I learned later in my life that if I would have taken away one process of my life by regretting , I would have taken away a part of me today.

So, you see, we need the good as well as the bad in order to keep achieving greater levels of success at this thing called life. At times we believe we are already mature enough to handle everything that comes our way only to fall by our own devices. But, when we allow God to be God, His process will mature us so that we are able to handle the next level of our lives.

Psalm 37: 9 says, For evildoers will be cut off, But those who <u>wait</u> for the Lord, they will inherit the land.

47

In the Hebrew language the word wait (qavah; kaw-vaw) means to stretch, tension of enduring, remain, wait in other words to mature, which takes the verb part of speech, action. It is important that we mature, grow in the grace and the knowledge of our Lord and Savior, Jesus Christ by allowing the Spirit of Truth to rest upon us and come alive in our lives. This process will not kill you, it will not take you out because remember, after all, that you have to live to tell someone else how you made it through.

You will allow God to do the work inside of you. You are an overcomer. You are an achiever and nothing can stop you now. There is no mountain high or wide enough that can stop you from maturing. Remember, he has brought you over and out! Out of what? you ask. Out of the lion's den but there was someone else there with you and He made a promise, **He will never leave you nor forsake you. Deuteronomy 31:6 (NIV)**.

Prayer of Agreement:

Lord, in the name of Jesus, I bless you. I honor you. I give you praise. Thank you for being Alpha and Omega in my life. Thank you for being the Everlasting King. In Jesus' name, Father, I ask that you forgive me for every place that I did not allow patience to have its perfect work in my life. Father, forgive me for the moments when I tried to rush the process; rush the mandate and tried to help you out in your plan for my life. Father, today I surrender my will, my plan, my emotions unto you. Amen

Reflection Scripture:

For evildoers will be cut off, But those who <u>wait</u> for the Lord, they will inherit the land. ~ *Psalm 37: 9*

My Personal Journal Notes:

_____

_____

_____

_____

_____

_____

_____

_____

_____

_____

_____

_____

_____

_____

_____

_____

_____

_____

_____

_____

_____

_____

_____

Signed: _____

Date: _____

My Personal Journal Notes:

_____

_____

_____

_____

_____

_____

_____

_____

_____

_____

_____

Signed: _____

Date: _____

My Personal Journal Notes:

_____

_____

_____

_____

_____

_____

_____

_____

_____

_____

_____

_____

_____

_____

_____

_____

_____

_____

_____

_____

_____

_____

_____

_____

_____

Signed: _____

Date: _____

CHAPTER 5

BE STEADFAST

My Dearest Daughter,

Remain steadfast in every good work that you do! I know sometimes, upon this journey, you will be faced with a lot of frustration but it is important that you remain steadfast and unmovable. Let me say it like this; remain steadfast upon the thing that is right in the will of God. Sometimes we can remain steadfast in things that do not give back to us. These things will take away from you and throw you completely off course.

To be steadfast simply means to be unwavering or loyal; fast fixed; firm; firmly fixed or established; to be constant; resolute; not fickle or wavering. I want you to be determined to work hard at improving yourself. I want you to be steadfast even when the odds seem to be stacked against you. There is a big difference between being headstrong or stubborn versus being steadfast.

Many times, you will find that Jesus uses many natural examples for us to understand spiritual things. Take the hawk for example. Hawks that fly in the midnight hours can see its way no matter the blackest of the night. Its path is made and its senses are intact. Amazingly, hawks can see and distinguish between colors. They have very sharp eyesight like all birds and they can see eight times better than humans can! Daughter, I believe just as God has made this wonderful creature to survive the most dangerous situations by using some of its special abilities, so do I believe that God has made us! As you go in and out of situations of life you will remember that God has a plan for you. Stop getting lost in that place where only anxiety, stress and complacency reside.

Daughter, while the midnight may seem as black as a thousand nights, you are to use your gift of sight to understand the will and plan for your life. Giving up is not an option. Do not stop…you are to keep moving. Do not walk when you should be running. Do not sleep when you are supposed to be awake. Where has your drive gone? What are you doing? Who told you your dream was dead? Why have you given up? You must get up and begin again. It is vital that you remain steadfast.

Life will be full of many ups and downs, losses and gains, joys and many sad times but let your drive push past the pressure by remaining steadfast in life's journey. As you begin to strike out again, life will try to teach you many lessons. I pray that you will gain the many lessons of hope, redemption, faith, love, sacrifice and humility that are found only in God. Do not allow your current situation bring you to faithlessness. Do not allow your emotional state of mind to overwhelm your spiritual intelligence. There should be a place within you that is perpetual; a place where faith never ceases and is never conquered, even as it is tested.

Daughter, keep your footing, be steadfast and unmovable no matter what or whoever comes against you. You have this! You are already an overcomer. Your selfless act of love does not match your low performance of faith right now. Get it together! Make great strives right here! Stop remaining at the banks of life and ask the Father to call you deeper. Elijah made the decision to continue past his limitation, trusting and believing that God has already paved the way. Yes, I desire to get into the personal space of your life right now…the life that you check in to and out of. Pick up your bags of comfortability and move to a place of faith and trust. Even at this time it may seem that you are knee deep but remain steadfast by trusting that He has a plan that is just for you.

Sometimes life wants to throw us around and feed us to a mass of sharks that would be glad to consume us from head to toe. I would be remiss to lead you in believing that I do not know or understand what it means to be steadfast even when the odds are stacked against you. Yes, I do know and understand whole-heartedly. Sometimes you are plagued with thoughts of giving up. If that plan did not work for me yesterday, why would I believe it will work today? Sometimes you are plagued with emotions of void and disappointment within yourself. Sometimes you are challenged with completing what you have started. The fear of failure may arise but just as you are bombarded with millions of these thoughts, here comes a strength that is greater than your own that will cause you to keep moving.

The bible says, in *1 Peter 5:9, Whom resist steadfast in the faith, knowing that the same afflictions are accomplished in your brethren that are in the world.* Remember that God will never leave you alone. He will always send something or someone in your path to help encourage you. The best example I have is a dog's undying devotion to his master, steadfast.

Prayer of Agreement:

Lord, in the name of Jesus, I honor you. I give you glory. Thank you Lord for you are the constant, the consistency in my life that I need. I thank you for always being who you are. You are the Great I Am. You are the Great Perpetuator, you are the Advocator. God, you are my Vindicator and I thank you right now in the name of Jesus. Father, forgive me for the times that I have given up and fell short of your glory. God, I fell short of the plan that you have for my life because I got a little impatient and I got fearful or let the naysayer, the backbiter, and life situations come in and stop me. But, God, today I make a vow before you and in the presence of the Host of Angels that I will remain steadfast, immovable, abounding in your works. I shall be like that tree planted by the rivers of water and I shall bring forth fruit in my season even though the winds and the billows may roar. Father, I will do as Peter did and step out of the boat even though the winds may be boisterous and moving upon the calmness of the sea. Father, but at the calling of the name of Jesus, I will be steadfast in the work that you have called me to do. Father, I will be consistent. I will be persistent in what you have put at my hands to do. God, I will not turn away from the plan or the call. God, I thank you because you could have called so many others yet, you called me. So God, today I vow my life unto you in Jesus' name I pray. *Amen*

Reflection Scripture:

Count it all joy, my brothers, when you meet trials of various kinds, for you know that the testing of your faith produces steadfastness. ~ **James 1:2**

My Personal Journal Notes:

_____

_____

_____

_____

_____

_____

_____

_____

_____

_____

_____

_____

_____

_____

_____

_____

_____

_____

_____

_____

_____

_____

_____

_____

Signed: _____

Date: _____

My Personal Journal Notes:

_____

_____

_____

_____

_____

_____

_____

_____

_____

_____

_____

_____

_____

_____

_____

_____

_____

_____

_____

_____

_____

_____

_____

_____

Signed: _____

Date: _____

My Personal Journal Notes:

_____

_____

_____

_____

_____

_____

_____

_____

_____

_____

Signed: _____

Date: _____

CHAPTER 6

EMOTIONAL HOARDING

My Dearest Daughter,

An emotional hoarder is a person who is more committed to sorrow than joy. In this place you have lost your own identity to suffering and self-loathing. Blinded by emotions of pain, you could never see the joy. This person is stricken by an epidemic that is holding their joy hostage and robbing them of their fulfillment (Huffington Post).

If you find yourself collecting, keeping, packing, tucking away any and everything emotional that has transpired in your life from year to year, yes, you are guilty of being an emotional hoarder. An emotional hoarder stores every traumatic memory, slight, embarrassment, and heartbreak, past and present, only to live with the burden of each one every day. This condition will cause one to become withdrawn from family, friends and the world.

Emotional scarring I find is the worst of all that you would have to deal with in your life. Emotions are like a central nervous system to bondage. It has a place where forgiveness, hidden desires lurk, and bad and good memories are stored. It has a closet door to close up all the pain that you try to hide and keep out of the sight of people hoping that no one will notice the change in you.

Daughter, you are not alone! It is time to clean out the

closet by facing the painful feelings of your emotions...the feeling of rejection, disappointment, broken heartedness, highly stressful situations, death of a sufficient person in your life, empty nest syndrome, etc.

Let us put our emotions in check. Do you remember Linus on Charlie Brown with blanket? He had to have it everywhere he went, whether clean or dirty. I know by now in your life you have been through a lot so at the very thought of you letting go of things that you may have collected, packed, tucked, it seems impossible to let it go. However, you *must*. You *must* become the overcomer. You *must* be willing to overcome the pain of the loss of the loved one(s).

You have compartmentalized your life long enough. Now, it has come time for you to live a whole and free life from the entanglements and bondages that have been brought into your life. It is time to get busy living and stop dying in that place of pain and misery. You have the power to overcome it and to get rid of any and everything that has tried to hold you bound. How many of the following items still tries to keep you under arrest?

Low self-esteem, hurt of any kind, lying ,cheating, misfortune, loss, drama, career loss, heartbreak, failed accomplishment(s), lost goals, shattered dreams, loss of direction, embarrassment

All of these emotions mixed with fear and anxiety comes along with control and the need to collect those things that one has lost.

Daughter, no more collecting emotions of the past. Now, it is time to move forward!

Prayer of Agreement:

Father, in the name of Jesus, I come to you and give you glory. Holy is thy name for you are worthy to be praised. Thank you always and forever. Father, I ask that you forgive me for each time I have collected things of the past and I have allowed them to haunt my present, dismissing my future. Father, right now in the name of Jesus, I let go of the pain of my past, of a broken heart, of loss, of disappointment. Father, I let go of all the old things that have tried to cause stumbling blocks. I've allowed many things to pile up behind the doors of my heart where you need to be and the doors have slammed shut. Father, today I ask that you come into my life and remove the clutter of yesterday... the clutter of hate... the clutter of anger... the clutter of bitterness... the clutter of disappointment... the clutter of old wasted places... the clutter that has caused us to be neither consistent nor persistent. God, I have allowed these things to cloud my judgment and eyesight to where the hills of life have tried to overtake me. I thank you today for the redemptive plan of yours. You have a plan that is set for me. God, I open the doors of my heart by kicking down the doors disappointment by bursting in and knocking down walls. God, thank you that you are the one who will take the doors off the hinges that will try and bind us.

Father, right now, I confess that the spirit of emotional hoarding have tried to overtake me. I command the fear of loneliness to go. I command the fear of entrapment and the spirit of trauma to go right now in the name of Jesus. Amen

Reflection Scripture:

I have seen a grievous evil under the sun: wealth hoarded to the harm of its owners. ~ ***Ecclesiastes 5:13***

My Personal Journal Notes:

_____

_____

_____

_____

_____

_____

_____

_____

_____

_____

_____

Signed: _____

Date: _____

My Personal Journal Notes:

_____

_____

_____

_____

_____

_____

_____

_____

_____

_____

_____

_____

Signed: _____

Date: _____

My Personal Journal Notes:

_____

_____

_____

_____

_____

_____

_____

_____

_____

_____

_____

_____

_____

_____

_____

_____

_____

_____

_____

_____

_____

_____

_____

_____

Signed: _____

Date: _____

My Personal Journal Notes:

_____

_____

_____

_____

_____

_____

_____

_____

_____

_____

_____

Signed: _____

Date: _____

CHAPTER 7

Someday you may want to leave letters/journals for your loved ones. I am providing a place for you to begin.

_____

_____

(Title Your Story)

Prayer of Agreement:

_____

_____

_____

_____

_____

_____

_____

_____

_____

_____

Reflection Scripture:

_____

_____

Dear _____

_____

_____

_____

_____

_____

_____

_____

_____

_____

_____

_____

_____

Signed: _____

Date: _____

CHAPTER 8

_____

_____

(Title Your Story)

Prayer of Agreement:

_____

_____

_____

_____

_____

_____

_____

_____

_____

Reflection Scripture:

_____

_____

Dear _____

_____

_____

_____

_____

_____

_____

_____

_____

_____

_____

_____

_____

_____

_____

_____

_____

_____

_____

_____

_____

_____

_____

Signed: _____

Date: _____

CHAPTER 9

_____

_____

(Title Your Story)

Prayer of Agreement:

_____

_____

_____

_____

_____

_____

_____

_____

_____

_____

Reflection Scripture:

_____

_____

Dear _____

_____

_____

_____

_____

_____

_____

_____

_____

_____

_____

_____

_____

_____

_____

_____

_____

_____

_____

_____

_____

_____

_____

_____

_____

Signed: _____

Date: _____

CHAPTER 10

_____

_____

(Title Your Story)

Prayer of Agreement:

_____

_____

_____

_____

_____

_____

_____

_____

Reflection Scripture:

_____

_____

Dear _____

_____

_____

_____

_____

_____

_____

_____

_____

_____

_____

_____

_____

_____

_____

_____

_____

_____

_____

_____

_____

_____

_____

_____

Signed: _____

Date: _____

ABOUT THE AUTHOR

Prophetess Lady Schowanda Michael was consecrated into the office of Prophetess in 2009 and ministers alongside her husband, Apostle Dr. Cardell A. Michael. She is the mother of four.

Lady Michael birthed the Women of Power (WOP) Ministry of Higher Heights in 2010. In 2011, she began a mentor program that targets the Kingdom Mind of a Woman. Lady Michael's vision is to empower women, whether young or old, to become vessels that God can use in their season.

She is the founder of the LAY'D (Living and Achieving Your Destiny) brand in which she encourages and reminds women that through all that life brings, that they are to be steadfast in their walk with God. Lady Michael is the Spiritual Mother to several women in ministry through her mentor program, Women in Ministry (WIM). Meetings for her mentor program, Women of Worth (WOW) are held outside of the church where all women are welcome to attend.

Lady Michael believes that with the understanding of God's Holy Word, that all women can and will be Women of Power NOT just in word but in lifestyle!

Made in the USA
Columbia, SC
07 November 2024

45911401R00061